John Cabot

Steven Roberts

PowerKiDS
press

New York

Published in 2013 by The Rosen Publishing Group, Inc.
29 East 21st Street, New York, NY 10010

Copyright © 2013 by The Rosen Publishing Group, Inc.

First Edition

Editor: Joanne Randolph

Book Design: Planman Technologies

Illustrations: Planman Technologies

Library of Congress Cataloging-in-Publication Data

Roberts, Steven, 1955-

John Cabot / by Steven Roberts. — 1st ed.

p. cm. — (Jr. graphic famous explorers)

Includes index.

ISBN 978-1-4777-0072-3 (library binding) — ISBN 978-1-4777-0129-4 (pbk.) — ISBN 978-1-4777-0130-0 (6-pack)

1. Cabot, John, d. 1499—Juvenile literature. 2. America—Discovery and exploration—British—Juvenile literature. 3. North America—Discovery and exploration—British—Juvenile literature. 4. Explorers—America—Biography—Juvenile literature. 5. Explorers—Great Britain—Biography—Juvenile literature. 6. Explorers—Italy—Biography—Juvenile literature. 7. Cabot, John, d. 1499—Comic books, strips, etc. 8. America—Discovery and exploration—British—Comic books, strips, etc. 9. North America—Discovery and exploration—British—Comic books, strips, etc. 10. Explorers—America—Biography—Comic books, strips, etc. 11. Explorers—Great Britain—Biography—Comic books, strips, etc. 12. Explorers—Italy—Biography—Comic books, strips, etc. 13. Graphic novels. I. Title.

E129.C1R63 2013

970.01'5092—dc23

[B]

2012018691

Manufactured in the United States of America

CPSIA Compliance Information: Batch # W13PK1: For Further Information contact Rosen Publishing, New York, New York at 1-800-237-9932

Contents

Introduction

The late 1400s marked the dawn of European exploration. Columbus discovered the New World, and the seafaring powers of Europe were competing to find new trade routes to Asia. England had not yet emerged as a sea power and was looking for an experienced **navigator**. It would find that man in John Cabot. The story of John Cabot, however, is one of the great mysteries of exploration. None of his maps or records have survived. What little we know about him has been pieced together by letters from his friends and the work of **historians**.

Main Characters

John Cabot (c. 1450–c. 1499) An Italian navigator and explorer. He sailed to what is today Newfoundland, Canada, becoming the first European to set foot in North America since the Vikings.

Mattea Cabot (c. 1460s–c. 1500s) John Cabot's wife, with whom he had three children.

Sebastian Cabot (c. 1476–1557) John Cabot's youngest son, who also became an explorer.

John Day (c. 1460s–c. 1500s) A **merchant** from Bristol, England, and friend of John Cabot. His letters are one of the sources of information about John Cabot's voyages.

Raimondo de Soncino (c. 1460s–c. 1500s) Served as the **ambassador** from Milan, Italy, to England and a friend of John Cabot. A letter he wrote is the main source of information about Cabot's most famous voyage.

King Henry VII (1457–1509) The king of England. He financed John Cabot's voyages.

Gaspar Corte Real (c. 1450–c. 1501) A Portuguese explorer who sailed to Canada a couple of years after Cabot.

JOHN CABOT

ALTHOUGH ENGLAND CLAIMS JOHN CABOT AS ITS FIRST GREAT EXPLORER, HE WAS NOT ENGLISH, AND HIS NAME WAS NOT JOHN CABOT. HE WAS BORN AROUND 1450 IN GENOA, ITALY. HIS REAL NAME WAS GIOVANNI CABOTO.

England

Portugal

France

Genoa

Italy

Spain

N
W   E
S

Mediterranean Sea

IN HIS LATE TEENS, GIOVANNI WORKED AS A MERCHANT. HE TRAVELED BY LAND TO MECCA, THE MUSLIM HOLY CITY, AND LEARNED THE TRADE ROUTES BETWEEN ASIA AND EUROPE.

SOON GIOVANNI BECAME A SAILOR. HE LEARNED THE TRADE ROUTES BETWEEN THE GREAT PORTS OF EUROPE ON THE MEDITERRANEAN SEA.

AS A SAILOR, GIOVANNI SERVED IN MANY POSITIONS, INCLUDING CAPTAIN'S **APPRENTICE**.

YOU ARE A QUICK LEARNER. YOU WILL DO WELL IN LIFE, GIOVANNI.

HE LEARNED HOW TO USE **NAUTICAL** INSTRUMENTS, SUCH AS THE **ASTROLABE** AND THE **QUADRANT**, AND BECAME A NAVIGATOR.

I WANT TO BE A NAVIGATOR, NOT JUST WORK ON A MERCHANT SHIP.

HE MARRIED A WOMAN NAMED MATTEA AND THEY HAD THREE SONS, LUDOVICO, SANCTO, AND SEBASTIANO.

WHAT ARE YOU DOING, DADDY?

I'M STUDYING. ONE DAY I'M GOING TO EXPLORE THE WORLD.

WHEN CHRISTOPHER COLUMBUS RETURNED FROM HIS FAMOUS VOYAGE IN 1492, THE SEAFARING POWERS OF EUROPE WERE EAGER TO SEND **MISSIONS** ACROSS THE OCEAN.

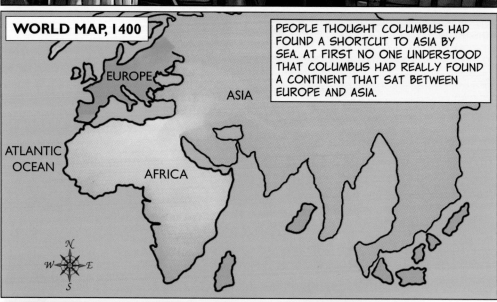

WORLD MAP, 1400

EUROPE

ASIA

ATLANTIC OCEAN

AFRICA

N W E S

PEOPLE THOUGHT COLUMBUS HAD FOUND A SHORTCUT TO ASIA BY SEA. AT FIRST NO ONE UNDERSTOOD THAT COLUMBUS HAD REALLY FOUND A CONTINENT THAT SAT BETWEEN EUROPE AND ASIA.

THE KING DID NOT EVEN LISTEN TO WHAT I HAD TO SAY.

THE KING IS NOT INTERESTED.

GIOVANNI CABOTO WAS EAGER TO EXPLORE AND FIND A NEW ROUTE TO ASIA. HE WENT TO SEE THE KINGS OF SPAIN AND PORTUGAL TO ASK THEM TO FINANCE A VOYAGE. BOTH KINGS TURNED HIM AWAY.

GIOVANNI CABOTO MOVED HIS FAMILY TO BRISTOL, ENGLAND. IT WAS ONE OF ENGLAND'S BUSIEST PORTS. THERE HE BECAME KNOWN AS JOHN CABOT.

MORNING, JOHN!

THE KING WILL SEE YOU NOW.

JOHN CABOT WENT TO SEE THE ENGLISH KING, HENRY VII, TO ASK HIM TO FINANCE A VOYAGE. THE KING WANTED TO SET UP NEW TRADE ROUTES TO ASIA, BUT ENGLAND DID NOT HAVE ANYONE WITH CABOT'S EXPERIENCE NAVIGATING ROUGH WATERS OR EXPLORING DISTANT LANDS.

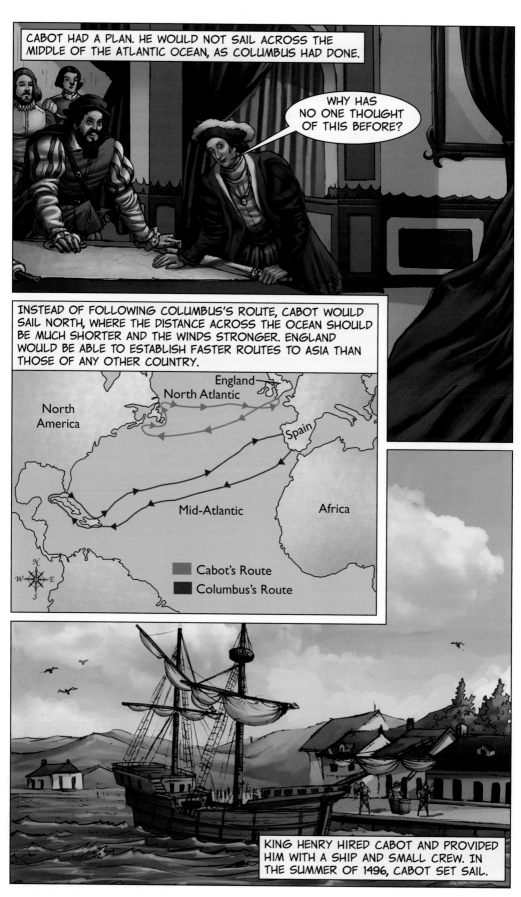

CABOT HAD A PLAN. HE WOULD NOT SAIL ACROSS THE MIDDLE OF THE ATLANTIC OCEAN, AS COLUMBUS HAD DONE.

WHY HAS NO ONE THOUGHT OF THIS BEFORE?

INSTEAD OF FOLLOWING COLUMBUS'S ROUTE, CABOT WOULD SAIL NORTH, WHERE THE DISTANCE ACROSS THE OCEAN SHOULD BE MUCH SHORTER AND THE WINDS STRONGER. ENGLAND WOULD BE ABLE TO ESTABLISH FASTER ROUTES TO ASIA THAN THOSE OF ANY OTHER COUNTRY.

England
North Atlantic
North America
Spain
Mid-Atlantic
Africa

Cabot's Route
Columbus's Route

KING HENRY HIRED CABOT AND PROVIDED HIM WITH A SHIP AND SMALL CREW. IN THE SUMMER OF 1496, CABOT SET SAIL.

CABOT DID NOT GET FAR. WHAT LITTLE IS KNOWN OF THIS VOYAGE IS FROM A LETTER WRITTEN BY HIS FRIEND JOHN DAY TO CHRISTOPHER COLUMBUS.

YOUR LORDSHIP, HERE IS WHAT HAPPENED AS **RELATED** TO ME BY CAPTAIN CABOT.

SOON AFTER HE SET OUT TO SEA, CABOT'S SHIP RAN INTO BAD WEATHER.

HE WILL GET US ALL KILLED!

HE IS NOT EVEN ENGLISH! WE CAN'T TRUST HIM.

THE CREWMEN, WHO HAD NEVER SAILED INTO UNKNOWN WATERS BEFORE, BECAME FRIGHTENED AND TURNED AGAINST CABOT.

CABOT TURNED THE SHIP AROUND AND RETURNED TO PORT.

ALL MY WORK AND PLANNING WASTED. HOW COULD THIS HAVE HAPPENED?

KING HENRY STILL HAD CONFIDENCE IN CABOT AND DECIDED TO FINANCE A SECOND VOYAGE.

FOR KING AND COUNTRY, YOUR HIGHNESS. I WILL NOT FAIL THIS TIME.

WE MUST TRY AGAIN, JOHN.

CABOT WAS GIVEN A THREE-MASTED SHIP CALLED THE *MATTHEW*, A CREW OF 18 ABLE SEAMEN, AND ENOUGH SUPPLIES TO LAST FOR SEVERAL MONTHS.

WE'RE WITH YOU, CAPTAIN!

MEN, DO YOU HAVE WHAT IT TAKES? IT WILL BE A LONG, HARD VOYAGE.

AYE, CAPTAIN!

THE *MATTHEW* SET SAIL FROM BRISTOL, ENGLAND, ON MAY 22, 1497.

THIS TIME, CABOT WOULD NOT RISK FAILING. HE SAILED FIRST TO THE COAST OF IRELAND AND DROPPED ANCHOR. THERE HE TOOK READINGS OF HIS POSITION AND THE WEATHER, USING HIS INSTRUMENTS AND OBSERVING THE NORTH STAR.

CAN I GET YOU ANYTHING, CAPTAIN?

FAIR SKIES AND FAIR WINDS ARE ALL I WANT.

AFTER GAINING HIS **BEARINGS**, CABOT SET OUT INTO UNKNOWN WATERS.

BECAUSE NO RECORD OF CABOT'S VOYAGE EXISTS, HISTORIANS CAN ONLY GUESS WHAT IT WAS LIKE. AS HE CROSSED THE ICY WATERS OF THE NORTH ATLANTIC, CABOT WOULD HAVE FACED HEAVY WINDS AND SAILED AROUND ICEBERGS.

PULL STARBOARD, MEN!

WE'RE CLEAR OF ICE, AT LEAST FOR NOW.

STEADY AS SHE GOES.

IT WOULD HAVE TAKEN ALL HIS SKILLS AS A NAVIGATOR TO SAIL THROUGH THE DENSE NORTH ATLANTIC FOG.

AFTER OVER A MONTH AT SEA, CABOT ARRIVED IN NORTH AMERICA.

LAND HO!

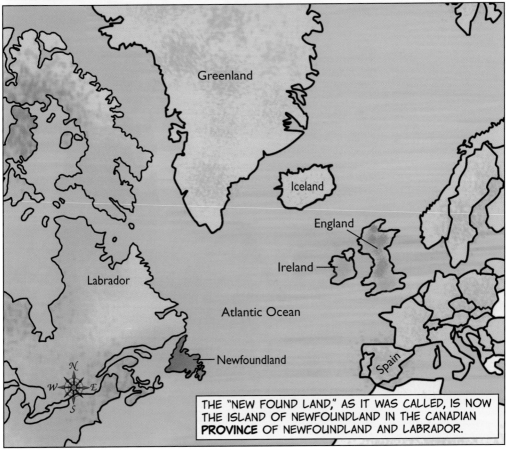

CABOT AND HIS CREW EXPLORED THE SHORE AND FOUND SIGNS OF NATIVE LIFE. THEY FOUND THE REMAINS OF A CAMPFIRE AND A TRAIL LEADING INLAND.

THIS LAND IS INHABITED.

WHO KNOWS WHAT WE WILL FIND? THESE PEOPLE COULD KILL US.

NOT KNOWING WHETHER THE NATIVES WOULD BE FRIENDLY OR **HOSTILE**, HE DID NOT WANT TO RISK THE LIVES OF HIS CREW. HE ORDERED HIS MEN BACK ABOARD THE SHIP. THIS WAS THE ONLY TIME CABOT SET FOOT ON LAND.

WE MUST NOT TAKE ANY CHANCES.

FOR THE NEXT FEW WEEKS, CABOT EXPLORED THE EASTERN COAST OF CANADA AND MAPPED HIS FINDINGS, THINKING HE HAD REACHED THE NORTHEAST COAST OF ASIA. HE SAW DENSE FORESTS AND SIGNS OF NATIVE VILLAGES.

THE SEA WAS SWARMING WITH FISH. THERE WERE SO MANY THAT THE MEN COULD CATCH THEM SIMPLY BY LOWERING BASKETS INTO THE WATER.

HIS MISSION COMPLETE, CABOT HEADED FOR HOME. THE *MATTHEW* ARRIVED BACK IN BRISTOL, ENGLAND, ON AUGUST 6, 1497. HIS SHIP WAS **INTACT**, AND CABOT HAD NOT LOST A SINGLE MEMBER OF HIS CREW.

CABOT IMMEDIATELY TOOK A COACH TO LONDON TO MEET WITH KING HENRY VII. THE COACH RIDE TOOK HIM THREE DAYS.

ENGLAND CANNOT PAY YOU ENOUGH.

IT IS MY HONOR TO SERVE YOU, YOUR HIGHNESS.

KING HENRY WAS EXCITED BY THE SUCCESS OF CABOT'S **EXPEDITION**. HE REWARDED CABOT WITH 10 POUNDS OF SILVER AND ANOTHER 20 POUNDS PER YEAR, WHICH WAS A VERY LARGE SUM IN THOSE DAYS.

THE WORLD IS NOW YOURS.

SPLENDID!

CABOT MADE A MAP AND A GLOBE OF HIS FINDINGS FOR THE KING. THE MAP AND GLOBE NO LONGER EXIST, NOR DO ANY RECORDS CABOT MADE OF HIS JOURNEY.

JOHN CABOT QUICKLY BECAME A NATIONAL HERO. HE WAS THE MAN WHO HAD DISCOVERED A NEW ROUTE TO ASIA FOR ENGLAND, OR SO THEY THOUGHT AT THE TIME.

ALL HAIL JOHN CABOT!

CABOT DESCRIBED HIS VOYAGE TO SEVERAL OF HIS FRIENDS. IT IS FROM THEIR LETTERS THAT WE KNOW ABOUT CABOT'S EXPERIENCES. ONE OF THOSE FRIENDS WAS RAIMONDO DE SONCINO, THE AMBASSADOR FROM MILAN, ITALY.

YOUR STORY IS MOST AMAZING.

IN A LETTER TO THE DUKE OF MILAN, SONCINO WROTE THAT CABOT "IS CALLED THE GREAT ADMIRAL AND GREAT HONOUR IS PAID TO HIM AND HE GOES DRESSED IN SILK. THE ENGLISH ARE READY TO GO WITH HIM."

AREN'T YOU THE GREAT ADMIRAL?

KING HENRY WAS EAGER TO SEND CABOT TO SEA AGAIN ON A MUCH LARGER EXPEDITION.

YOU SHALL HAVE 10 ARMED SHIPS AND ALL THE CREW YOU NEED.

THE KING, HOWEVER, WAS SPENDING TOO MUCH MONEY PUTTING DOWN **REBELLIONS** IN ENGLAND. AFTER MONTHS OF PLANNING, HE DECIDED HE COULD NOT AFFORD A LARGE-SCALE EXPEDITION AND GAVE CABOT ONLY ONE SHIP.

SOME OF THE MERCHANTS OF BRISTOL RAISED ENOUGH MONEY FOR FOUR MORE SHIPS.

WE SHALL MAKE A FORTUNE OFF THE NEW TRADE ROUTES.

IN THE SPRING OF 1498, CABOT SET SAIL ON HIS THIRD AND FINAL VOYAGE. THIS TIME HE WOULD NOT BE SO LUCKY.

CABOT FOLLOWED THE SAME ROUTE AS HE DID THE YEAR BEFORE. AFTER SETTING SAIL FROM IRELAND, THE SHIPS WERE CAUGHT IN A STORM. ONE OF THE SHIPS WAS BADLY DAMAGED AND HAD TO TURN BACK.

THE REST OF THE SHIPS SAILED ON AND WERE NEVER HEARD FROM AGAIN. BY 1499, CABOT AND HIS CREW HAD BEEN GIVEN UP FOR DEAD.

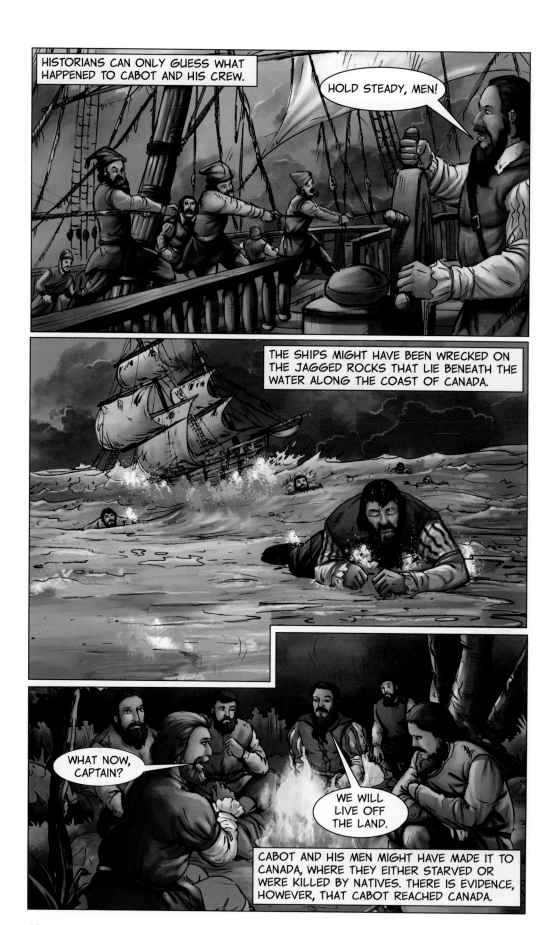

IN 1500, TWO YEARS AFTER CABOT'S FINAL VOYAGE, A PORTUGUESE EXPLORER NAMED GASPAR CORTE REAL SAILED TO CANADA. HE FOUND PART OF A SWORD AND SOME SILVER RINGS THAT COULD ONLY HAVE COME FROM CABOT'S HOME COUNTRY OF ITALY.

MANY YEARS LATER, IN 1526, ANOTHER GREAT EXPLORER SET SAIL TO NORTH AMERICA FOR SPAIN. HIS ENGLISH NAME WAS SEBASTIAN CABOT, THE YOUNGEST SON OF JOHN CABOT.

NO ONE WILL EVER REALLY KNOW WHAT BECAME OF GIOVANNI CABOTO, BUT HE EARNED HIS PLACE IN HISTORY AS JOHN CABOT, THE FIRST ENGLISHMAN TO REACH AMERICA.

Timeline and Map

c. 1450   John Cabot is born in Genoa, Italy, as Giovanni Caboto.

1474   Caboto marries Mattea. They have three sons named Ludovico, Sancto, and Sebastiano.

1492   Christopher Columbus sails the Atlantic Ocean and finds what he thinks is a new route to Asia.

1490s   Caboto goes to see the kings of Spain and Portugal to ask them to finance a voyage, but his requests are denied.

c. 1490–   Caboto moves his family to Bristol, England, where he
1495   becomes known as John Cabot.

1496   The English king, Henry VII, agrees to finance a voyage for Cabot. Cabot sets sail on his first voyage from Bristol. He does not get far and turns back.

1497   In May, Cabot sets sail on his second voyage from Bristol.

On June 24, Cabot arrives in what is now Newfoundland, Canada.

On August 6, Cabot arrives back in Bristol.

1498   In May, Cabot sets sail on his third voyage and is never seen again.

1500   Gaspar Corte Real, a Portuguese explorer, finds what might be the remains of Cabot's expedition.

1525   John Cabot's youngest son, Sebastian Cabot sails to the Americas in 1526.

Map of Cabot's Route

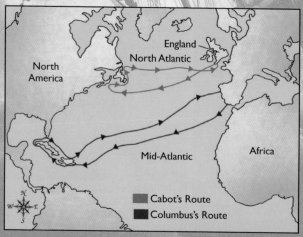

North America

England
North Atlantic

Mid-Atlantic

Africa

N
W · E
S

■ Cabot's Route
■ Columbus's Route

Glossary

ambassador (am-BA-suh-dur) The highest-ranking representative of one country assigned to conduct relations with another country.

apprentice (uh-PREN-tis) A person who learns a trade by working for someone who is already trained.

astrolabe (AS-truh-layb) An instrument that measures the positions of stars, used to find one's way on the oceans.

bearings (BER-ingz) Measurements taken that will tell the geographical position of a person or a thing.

expedition (ek-spuh-DIH-shun) A trip for a special purpose.

historians (hih-STOR-ee-unz) People who study the past.

hostile (HOS-tul) Unfriendly, relating to an enemy.

intact (in-TAKT) Not broken or damaged.

merchant (MER-chunt) Someone who owns a business that sells goods.

missions (MIH-shunz) Special jobs or tasks.

nautical (NAW-tih-kul) Relating to ships, navigation, and to sailing.

navigator (NA-vuh-gay-ter) A person who uses maps, the stars, or special tools to travel in a ship, an aircraft, or a rocket.

province (PRAH-vins) One of the main parts of a country.

quadrant (KWAH-drunt) An instrument for measuring the altitude of a star or of the Sun in order to find one's geographical position from the ocean.

rebellions (rih-BEL-yunz) Fights against one's government.

related (rih-LAYT-ed) Told something, such as a story.

Index

Websites

Due to the changing nature of Internet links, PowerKids Press has developed an online list of websites related to the subject of this book. This site is updated regularly. Please use this link to access the list:

www.powerkidslinks.com/jgff/cabo/